Troubled Women God Cares When You Are Hurting

By

Billie Green

ISBN: 1-4033-3221-5 (e-book)
ISBN: 1-4033-3222-3 (Paperback)

This book is printed on acid free paper.

1stBooks - rev. 09/22/03

I would like to thank…

I would like to thank all the people in my life that made this, my first book, possible through encouragement and great inspiration including: thank you to Selena Harris for her photography, Johnsy Brew for words of encouragement, Katey Dodson and Stephanie Hooten for inspiration, and Debra Ware and Dale Flemister and family for being friends when I needed them. I want to thank my mother Armeeda Reed and my father Bill Reed for all the times in my life when my needs were great and they provided me with beautiful roses and flowers on holidays that really kept me going. I would also like to give tribute and thanks to my wonderful husband and friend Jerry Casey Green who has been supportive and understanding.

Thank you also to my five wonderful children that the Lord has blessed me with.

Reference Guide

1. Troubled Women God cares in everything we do.
2. Troubled Women God has it all.
3. Troubled Women don't weep.
4. Troubled Women why God died for us.
5. Troubled Women, our souls, minds, and bodies belong to God.
6. Troubled Women raising teenage children.
7. Troubled Women battling divorce.
8. Troubled Women when life takes advantage, it's time to pray.
9. God will never leave you alone.
10. Troubled Women facing the loss of a child.
11. Troubled Women facing a addiction.

"Troubled Women, God Cares When You Are Hurting"

There are so many women hurting and coping with fears such as growing old and abandonment by husbands or loved ones. These women do not know whom to turn to for help. Many women turn to the streets in order to pay bills. What on earth is the world facing? Who can these women turn to for their needs? God is the answer to every woman's worries. Whether it is in times of crisis, insecurities, or hopelessness and feelings of lost dreams, God wants to solve all problems and heal all wounds.

Many women share a common fear of growing old. While aging is a part of life, the reality of it brings new fears of uselessness or losing a mate to a younger woman. In times of trouble, God will be there. God loves us and wants to heal our pain with His divine love and give us the strength to overcome whatever we are facing. He cares about our problems and wants to meet our needs.

Today, women are raising families on their own. Many women are joining the workforce and using their skills and education to make a better life for their children and themselves. We are searching for answers only God has. In providing for our children, we trouble ourselves wondering if we will have enough money to feed and shelter our families. God has a plan for every woman. God plan will lead us to His kingdom and righteousness, and all the things promised in his Word. We live in a real and demanding world. We need God in everything we do. We must be ready and equipped with God's love as our shield and his Word as our weapon. We must realize that we are at war. We must also realize that there is no trouble too hard or deep for God to understand and solve.

If we obeyed God, there would be far less teen pregnancy and drug and gang related violence. Troubled women, there is hope because God cares about you.

Many women today has dreams that they think they can't fulfill because they don't know where to start. They don't know how to overcome or cope with their problems. But I am here to share the good news that God cares and has a plan for your life. His plan is of no cost and gives everlasting love. God has the answers to all your problems and questions. God is always there when we need Him. When you want to seek Him, He's never far away. It is then the God makes Himself visible. When we pray, God hears our cries. When we repent, His holy light eliminates the shadows of our souls. God love is so great and divine that it gives us the strength to overcome our obstacles and solve our problems. With His spirit, God brings love, joy, peace and happiness.

Whether or not you know, or want to believe, rejection plays a huge part in our lives. God wants us to be happy. He wants us to praise Him for the wonderful things He does in our lives from the great to the small. He loves to see us happy as we fulfill His plan for us all. Each and every woman is faced with many trials in life, in which God is there and ready to help. All we need to do is call upon Him. We must accept His love as our strength and God words as our answers to life's dilemmas. For the Lord loves us so much that God had His one begotten Son to die so that we could live.

Every woman is special in the eyes of God. God has great concern for the things in our lives that cause us grief and feelings of hopelessness and despair. Each woman is like a flower waiting to blossom, and with God's love, we will never wither or die, for God's love replenishes us eternally.

There is a special reason for everyone's life. God has a unique need in each woman. You are Mother Earth. Whether or not you believe Genesis chapter 1, stating that in the beginning, God created the heaven and earth, women are symbolic for bearing fruit and bringing forth life. God gave us this gift because He knows we are important and wants to fill our hearts and souls with His presence and love. We must believe that nothing can

5

stand in our way because God must come first in everything we do in life. We must settle for nothing less. We have the best in God if we allow His will to rule over all our days.

There are so many women faced with problems that only God can handle. There are hardships we must face, and choices we must make. Good decisions can only be made using prayer. Making the right choice can be hard, but prayer can help and lead us in the right direction. There are so many women facing hardships such as when husbands walk out, or coping with rebellious children, but we must look to God for all the answers. Doing this will eliminate the thoughts of whether or not you did the right thing. God knows that we will face all these problems and more. He also knows our hearts and God is always present to help us when the load becomes too much to bear. God loves us when there is no one around, and God loves us when we are in an audience. We must be strong enough to love Him in the same way, regardless of ridicule and persecution. Only God can bring us out of our troubled times and we must not be afraid to look for Him.

Women, God understands you when it seems dark and you're feeling troubled and worried. He does not want us to be worried because of the sins in our pasts or the things we are currently facing. God wants to heal our pains. God wants us to read His words and take them as our strength. God wants to encourage all women. When it seems that nothing is possible, God wants us to remember that all things are possible for all that love the Lord. Prayer changes things as well. God wants us to understand that and use it as our power and determination in pursuing our goals and desires. Worrying sometimes hinders us from praying about our problems and that's when the devil is at his most powerful. Satan then tries to bind us and prevent us from seeing God as our only true answer. But if we believe in God and fall on His words for strength, our circumstances will change and so will our lives because God cares.

Making good choices is key in life because they can bring great success to us. Good choices are essential now because we know this life will be ending soon. Everything we do should be helpful and, by making good decisions, we will be able to stand against the many tools of the devil. Our security is not in our children, our husbands, or in our jobs. Our security is in God. He is our friend, our confidante and our leader. God is closer to us than any relative and when we feel hopeless, don't be distraught, because He is with you. God is to be our shield and protector. Women, put your hope in God and wait to see what wonderful things God has in store for us. It may seem like a long time, but making good choices means good success and believing in the Lord is the best choice we can make.

Women, did you know that there is a hidden treasure that God has in every woman's life? There are many blessings in life that await those who obey God's will and allow Him to direct their steps. We concern ourselves with finding earthly treasures such as cars, houses and clothing, while missing the most important and obvious treasures of the joy and understand that only God can provide. Women, if you are faced with a problem, only God can solve it. Women, you can have it all. Whether they are the riches of the world or the wisdom of God, you can have all because God wants us to have it all. Because our Heavenly Father is rich and loving and caring. He is ready to answer you always.

I talk with so many women outside my surroundings that are troubled and hurting. They are trying to overcome the hardships and cope with life's problems alone. I ask God how I can help them. He told me to look within my heart and give my own triumphs as examples of God's abilities to heal anything. God wants to help us in our everyday lives and obtain favor in our hearts. By obtaining favor, God wants to be the one we choose to turn to for help and guidance. Mary was special because she was chosen to bear the child of God. Matthew chapter 1; verse 18 states how the birth of Jesus Christ was on this wise when as his mother Mary was espoused to Joseph.

Before they came together, she was found with child. She was blessed with what would be her hidden treasure.

Matthew chapter 2; verse 11 states *and when they were to come into the house, they saw the young child with Mary, his mother, and fell down and worshipped him. And when they had opened their treasures, they presented unto him gifts of gold and frankincense and myrrh.* Mary was being blessed because God knew she was a respectable person who obeyed Him. Obeying God's word can change our lives in ways we can't imagine, as it did Mary's. Though we will still face problems in life, we will not be brought down, for we have the ultimate answer.

What would we do if our health began to fail? Well, God has never failed us. Disease is just a word and a prayer away from being healed.

If you were in a life or death circumstance (situation), what would you do? The best thing for you to do would be to pray. Doctors try to help, but the truth is that without God, you are never really healed. The key to healing is within our hearts. If we believe in God, we make the necessary changes in our lives that keep us in good standing both physically and spiritually. Without faith, it is impossible to please God. Jesus says that faith the size of a mustard seed can move mountains. God wants to heal our bodies, minds and spirits of all ailments and troubles so that we can serve Him and mentor others in our lives. God cares about our physical, mental, spiritual and social health and wants to help.

Troubled women, God knows what's best for us. In life, we don't always know what's best. Some women feel as though having a good husband or a successful career is the number one goal in life. Pleasing God is the number one goal in life. Through doing so, you can only then experience what is best for Him and yourself. God has a blessing for all women at the door. It's up to us to accept it. At times, it may seem that the world is so large and complex that God doesn't notice your troubles. We must then have faith and use it as our determination to go in life because God is there with us all the way. We must believe and wait on the Lord's promise, as in the case of Hannah. Hannah wanted children, but the Lord shut up her womb. In that day, to have a child was a blessing because there were so many women that could not conceive children. Hannah prayed and prayed to God for a child, but she was infertile and unable to bear. But because of her faith and prayer, God obtained favor in her heart and His blessing was granted to her because she believed He would come through for her. Troubled women, don't lose hope. God knows what is best for your life. Don't let the materialistic things of this world become your sole reason for living. Put your lives in God's hands. The treasures of this world will not begin to compare to the riches of God kingdom for those who love God. You shall have them if you believe.

Troubled women, do not let beauty overrule your faith in God. I know there is beauty in all women. In our world, God made each and every woman beautiful in His sight and in our hearts. So let me take a journey with Esther. Queen Vash was a beautiful woman and the bible said Ester was to be brought to the King for him to behold her beauty. Esther would not let her beauty overrule her faith and loyalty to

God, even though she could have anything she wanted. Esther loved God. She depended on Him to get her through her tough times. She also knew that her people were in trouble. Because of her beauty, Esther gained the kindness of the King, though she accepted all of his offers of marriage. He was so overwhelmed by her, however, that he did eventually set her people free to please her. Esther never let anything come before God's place in her heart. For that, she and her people were rewarded.

Women, God must be in control of our lives. God has a plan for every woman's life. Whether we realize it or not, some of us may be called upon to teach, to lead or to nurture. For those of us that never reach our full potential in life, God still cares about where you stand and what you've accomplished. Every woman is a special person with a special place in God's heart. For the truly dedicated, there is also a special place for us in His kingdom.

Matthew chapter 19; verse 6 states: *wherefore they are no more twain, but one flesh. What therefore God hath joined together; let not man put asunder.* There are so many women searching for love for the wrong reasons. Some women look for relationships because they are lonely, insecure or need financial assistance. We need love in our lives at all times, not just when we feel at our lowest. In Matthew chapter 28; verse 20, Jesus says: *I am with you always. Even unto the end of the world.* That means a lot to me, even when I am lonely and things are not going my way. God will be with me. Every woman wants to be loved in the right way, and to gain God's love is to gain the best relationship imaginable. Once acquired, God's love is something no woman will want to lose. To all troubled women that seek a loving relationship, trust God and focus on His words. That will strengthen you and help you find true love and devotion.

Troubled women, we must obey God always. He wants to speak to us through our hearts and minds. As is stated in Genesis chapter 1; verse 1: *In the beginning, God created the heavens and the earth.* The first man, Adam, was created later as stated in Genesis chapter 2; verse 7. God gave Adam and Eve a chance at a life of perfection and happiness. They chose not to obey and were cast out of the Garden of Eden. We must choose to not stray from the word of God. For this, God will bless us. His word says that obedience is better than sacrifice, so let all people keep their minds and hearts open to God.

God came to the world and gave His only begotten son for us. Christ died so that we may have life and not perish. What greater love will we ever know? In St. Luke chapter 4; verse 18, Jesus says: *"the spirit of the Lord is upon me, because he hath anointed me to preach the gospel to the poor; he hath sent me to heal the brokenhearted, to preach deliverance to the captives."* Christ was sent by God to set us free. That is why He died.

Troubled women, our souls, minds and bodies belong to God. It says in Matthew chapter 4; verse 1: *then Jesus was led of the spirit into the wilderness to be tempted of the devil.* Jesus fasted for forty days and nights and was fatigued. Jesus' faith in His Father's word was so strong that even in His most vulnerable state, He was not weakened by temptation. Upon being tempted by Satan,

Jesus replied that no man lives by bread alone, but by the word of God. We must make our hearts and minds just like Jesus and think and act as Christ would, as the term *Christian* truly implies.

Troubled women, it can be very hard raising children around their troublesome teenage years. Prayer for our children is necessary. The word of God says we should train our children unto the Lord while they're young so that when they get older, they will not stray from Him. When we raise our children with God in their lives, we make them stronger against temptation and more appreciative of life's many small blessings. We must also keep God in our lives and make that visible to our children so that they may learn from our examples.

Divorce is a crisis that many women face. It can be so hard because of the need for human companionship. God wants us to experience love, not only from Him, but from other people as well. Battling divorce is never an easy thing to do in life, but we must realize that our lives will continue afterward. We must always look for a higher calling in life and keep our minds on God and His words and His promise.

When we go through life, it can take advantage of us and the everyday stress can take its toll. As always, it's time to pray. We must remember that prayer has the power to change even the most complicated situations. Doctors report that about 70% of patients that have undergone surgery successfully recover from ailments after praying for healing. Troubled women, when life's obstacles seem overbearing, look to God for the way around them. With God in your heart, you can win all your battles and make necessary changes to avoid them in the future. Our Heavenly Father loves us very much and wants to be a part of our lives.

God will never leave us alone or forsake us. Our Heavenly Father holds the answers to all our problems and questions. God wants to give us everlasting life, which can only be achieved through Him. God promises to be with us until the end of the world. Troubled women, do not feel that you are alone in this world. You are never alone. God is with all of us. He is even with those who don't acknowledge Him. God gave His only begotten son so that we could have everlasting life and a second chance at pleasing Him.

There are many sorrows and pains we must go through in life, but we do not bear them alone. God will supply our needs in life. God knows just how much we can handle and God will not put more on us. There is no wound too deep for the Lord's healing hand, and we must learn to turn our lives over to Him even in the darkest of times. God feels our pains and sorrows when we lose our children, for they are truly a gift from the moment they are born. The death of a child can have a tremendous impact on our hearts, but the Lord is there to comfort us and give us the strength to move on in life.

To the women in prison, my heart goes out to you. There may come times in life when it seems words cannot help, but prayer has the power to lighten even the most troubled spirit. We must also remember that the deeds of our past can be forgiven. What we do for Christ will bear an everlasting mark on our souls. Putting God first in our lives is what God wants. Doing this will bring us contentment. We should also remember that a trial in life is only a test to see how devoted and faithful we are in the Lord.

There are so many women hurting from battles with drug abuse. They look for help outside, but only God can truly heal them. Sometimes the emotional troubles of drugs can outweigh the physical pains of withdrawal and addiction. What these women do not realize is that healing of the body is of the least concern in this case. We need God to cleanse our minds and spirits. Only after this is done can the body begin to heal. We must remember that God is our shield and He wants us to cast our problems and cares to Him, for His love conquers all.

Troubled women, it's true that God loves you very much. What greater honor is there than to be called a child of God? To me, that is real love; for someone to lay down His life for others. God's love is divine and pure and as gentle as a dove. Try God's love. It costs absolutely nothing and there is everything to gain.

Insecurity can play a big part in our lives. God's word can make us feel secure about all things in our lives. Everybody likes to feel safe and loved, as we felt in our days of infancy. Without God's love, insecurity can bring jealousy, bitterness and anger, and life can seem worthless. God paid the price to make our lives worthwhile when He sent His only begotten son to die on the cross. God healed us through the wounds of Christ and by His stripes we are healed. Fears of insecurity play a role in our lives. Troubled women, we should pray daily and ask God for peace in our lives and for Him to take all our fears away. Let God

Holy Spirit overshadow us with His love and saving grace.

Troubled women, feelings of hopelessness can lead us to thinking that everything is coming at you instead of to you. God says that peace, joy and happiness are only a prayer away. Troubled women, don't feel like life is over for you because you are very special to God, who is our Heavenly Father. God cares when we are sad. God wants us to be happy in Him because He is everything to us. Troubled women, don't you know we are better than angels? When we die in Christ, our bodies are made equal to God. I know that feeling hopeless can make it seem as though no one cares, but keep in mind that God cares as much about us when we are sad as when we are happy.

Overcoming our problems can be very difficult because we are faced with problems and the world is full of them. But our problems can become less prominent if we obey God's words. Some of the problems we face have been brought on by our own actions, that is okay because God said if we never experience problems, we never truly know how God is the one and only solution. That is good news for me because I know God is on my side. I can look to God and depend on Him in everything I do. I know I have never been alone because God has always been with me. So, troubled women, you can overcome your problems if you allow God to intervene and take control of your life, as is said in His promise.

Troubled women, God wants to cleanse our minds and give us pure hearts. God does not want our bodies to be defiled by temptation and evil, but wants to fill our bodies and spirits with His holiness. One of the hardest parts of life can be letting go and fully depending on God. We should renew our minds and spirits in Him every day. God loves us and made sacrifices for us so that we may have life on earth and in heaven. We must trust God for our souls, minds and bodies belong to Him.

As we go through life, sometimes things can seem to take advantage of us. Prayer can change things and bring about peace. The more praying we do, the more changes and hope we get in return. In prayer, we ask God for answers. God returns them to us in blessings for believing in Him. We must look to God for peace that passes all understanding. We must hold on to our dreams troubled women. When life tries to grab and take advantage of us, God's healing hand and witness His compassion and grace.

Every woman has the fear of growing old. We wonder if our beauty will fade away. Well, the good news is that God loves us just the way we are and He says He will be with us when our hair turns gray. God never changes and neither does His words. God is the same yesterday as God is today. He is worthy of our trust and not hard to please. Remember, troubled women, growing old is not always easy, but it is part of life. We must realize that it is part of God's promise that He will never leave us alone if we believe in Him.

Trying to stay focused on God can be hard sometimes. We must remember that whoever keeps his mind on God will be kept in perfect peace. We must put God's words in front of our lives and make Him first in everything we do. There are so many things to be overburdened with in life. Chores such as cleaning and getting the children off to school can consume our minds and make us lose focus. Prayer helps us to keep our situations in perspective and God first. Keeping a song in our minds, praise in our hearts, and even talking and listening to other Christians are good ways to keep God in front of our lives.

Troubled women, we often wonder how we are going to feed our families. The struggle of living alone can be quite tremendous. God can supply all of our needs according to His riches and glory. The words of God speak to our hearts through faith. God will fulfill His promise, so worry not. All we need to do is believe in the promise of God.

The Lord loves a cheerful giver and God would never, and will not, forget your labors of love. You may be walking and find twenty dollars or someone may give you a house. You may also inherit money from an unknown source. This is the kind of God we serve. Keep that in mind, troubled women, and God will meet all your needs.

Yes, troubled women, you are stronger because our spirits can overcome our flesh. We could allow the devil to rule our lives through our thoughts, God came to set us free from our bad ways of thinking. Only if we let God in our hearts will our minds rule our flesh instead of having our flesh ruling our minds. God has a purpose for us in life. Let our strength lie in God and witness Him prove that we are stronger than anything the devil can throw at us. Troubled women, let your minds be one with God like Christ's was. God is our shield and nothing is impossible for Him.

Troubled women, don't let the cares of this life deceive you or rob you through artificial love. Every woman wants real love, but they look in the wrong direction. True love is hard to find in mortal men. Being betrayed can easily happen to anyone, God has a plan for every woman. We must first make the best decision, which is to follow God's word. We are to trust God in every way and if we obey His words, we will find true love in God. His love is a love that is free and priceless all the time. But more importantly, we will never be betrayed.

Troubled women, living alone is a battle we must cope with. Fear is hard when no one understands your worries. But God understands everything we face in life. When we think we are alone, we are not. God wants us to trust Him in everything we do. Praying brings us closer to God and knowing Him comforts us in times of sorrow. God comforts us when we are alone and that is a part of trust. That is goods news to me, so troubled women, remember you are not alone. God is with every woman whether they believe or not. He is there to wipe away all the troubles and tears. God loves you and cares.

Hardships bring disappointments, hurt and pain. They are part of the struggle of day-to-day living for all people. God knows each and every person's path in life. God said He knows how much we can bear and will put no more than that on us. We must remember to praise God for His faith in us to overcome our obstacles, even though we may suffer. God cares about our troubles and nothing is too hard for Him to deal with and understand. Prayer changes things and situations.

Remember that and we can outlast any hardship.

Troubled women, putting your hopes in God can bring testing in our jobs, surroundings, or even our own homes. Having a disbelieving spouse can be a difficult trial in life, you can overcome it. One of the greatest trials of life is waiting on God, since sometimes we try to do everything by ourselves. Life can take advantage of us, God says He will never leave or forsake us. That which He promises He will keep. His word says that if the husband does not believe in Him, then let him depart. Troubled women, ask God for the peace of mind that passes all understanding. God will give you the desire of your heart. Put your whole trust in God, even when you are faced with a disbelieving husband.

Remember that God has the answers to all your problems. No one said that life would be easy, God said that He would see us through the good times and the bad. Remember that you are special and seek the many hidden treasures in life. I want every woman to be encouraged and remember that you are not alone in the world. You are like a city set on God's hill. Let God wisdom shine through you and watch your troubles fade away like shadows from the sun. May God bring you the best of this life and everlasting life to come.

Recovering from childhood tragedies such as molestation can be hard. It is unfortunate that some of us encounter such violations in life. God can help us overcome our bad experiences and the fears of social rehabilitation. His love has the power to patch our wounds and mend our broken hearts.

Praying and asking God to help let go of our pain and fear is the key to total healing. We must keep a close relationship with Him for there is no problem too big for God's healing hand.

Troubled women, God planted a seed in every woman's heart. Just like apple seeds bring forth apples and orange seeds bring forth oranges, the seed of God brings out the part of Him placed in each of us. His love is like a flower that forever blooms. If we fail to nourish our seed with the word of God, we lose sight of the precious gift inside of us and the fruit it brings forth.

Jealousy is a powerful tool that the devil uses against us. If we pray and keep God first in our hearts, we need not worry about the evil thoughts that can sometimes enter our minds. Remember God's promise. Do not let the flesh rule the spirit and God will send His angels to protect us as we walk His path.

Troubled women, God will be with you step by step down any road. Sometimes we get so caught up in life's journey that we lose sight of our goals. If we take life one day at a time, we see the many blessings God has plans out for us. God loves us very much and wants us to have patience and believe in Him. True faith allows us to wait on God's promise that may take a day, a month or a year, but is always on time.

Troubled women, God does not change. Sometimes the pains we go through in life are not only trials, blessings within themselves. Some of these situations turn out to be the best solutions. God knows what is best and provides for us. God also knows what is in our hearts and what little we know about life. The changes we make for the better are never too late because God's love is always around us. He is our creator, and will keep us in perfect peace as long as we keep trust in Him.

There are lots of women struggling with bad past relationships and childhood experiences that prevent them from living complete lives. Many more fear and disorders that may occur later in life because of their life traumas. Know that God is always available to cure your pain and open your eyes to the rest of the world around you. Overcoming life's injustices can be very difficult, but we must become aware of the joy of life itself and the beauty of God's promise to us all.

Troubled women, God has a crown for you. He has crowns for all people that love Him. Those who allow God's Holy Spirit into their hearts and souls will receive God's gifts. He will cleanse our hearts of all our desires to do wrong and supply our needs. It is not hard giving up the things that keep us away from God, but the first part is letting go of our vices. God is never far away. God wants us to surrender our will to Him so that we may gain treasures far greater than that of any earthly possession.

Troubled women, God has a plan for your salvation. He is calling for a new birth. St. John chapter 3 recalls Nicodemus asking Jesus about being reborn. St. John chapter 3; verse 5 says, *"verily, verily, I say unto thee, Except a man be born of water and the Spirit, he cannot enter the kingdom of God."* Troubled women, it is not too hard or too late to receive God's blessings and follow God plan. God is calling for us to be filled with Him in this hour. Acts chapter 2; verse 17 says, *"and it shall come to pass in the last days, saith God, I will pour out my Spirit upon all flesh; and your sons and your daughters shall prophesy, and your young men shall see visions, and your old men shall dream dreams."*

Troubled women, God has a plan for your salvation. Acts chapter 2, verse 1 says, *"and the day of Pentecost was fully come, they were one accord in one place."* Verse 4 says, *"and they were filled with the Holy Ghost and began to speak with other tongues".* Verse 5 says, *"and they were dwelling at Jerusalem, Jews, devout men, out of every nation."*

Billie Green

A Moment to Remember
When I think of the time
we share together
in many special ways
and many kind words
God was always in the
midst of our company.

Billie Green

Faith keeps me
day by day reaching out.
My vision means more to me
than silver and gold.
Every day with Jesus
Is more wonderful
than the day before.

Women of victory
that win all the way.
There's never a battle
that loses the game.
God's peace and love
is with you all the way.
Women of victory
may your power endure
mightily each and every day.

A Poem From My Heart
What great wisdom
comes from Heaven above.
God's grace fall
upon each of us.
God's love is so rich,
so wonderful, so kind,
so divine.
I feel all God's wisdom,
that comes from Heaven above.

Lord, please take my sadness away.
I put all my burdens on the Lord and
He makes my day nice and
peaceful in every way.

Billie Green

Women of Vision That Never Fades Away
God puts a very special vision
in every woman's heart to stay.
Please always pray, don't let your
vision fade away.
If you keep the faith,
God will always have blessings
flowing your way.
It's only a test
that will soon pass away,
women of vision keep the faith
and have a blessed day.

Sacrificing Women
Denying herself always,
God has a plan fasting and praying.
Open your heart to let
God's love flow in.
Sacrificing women, it's a blessing
to please the Lord.

Billie Green

Women of Meditation
Meditate of God day and night,
it's like medication for your soul.
Having God's spirit is nice,
there is no refill,
you will always be filled.
There's never a price
women of meditation,
stay on your knees and
pray every night.

Women of Crown
There is a crown
that is coming your way.
There is a price that you
will have to pay your heavenly
father has made a way
you're only running a race.
The crown is made full of
gold, pearl and stone.
Women of crown,
it's not very far.

Billie Green

Enduring Women
Your work never ends,
God's work fills your day.
There are blessings flowing your way.
Keep the faith and have a happy day.
There is no mountain too high
to climb, so keep a happy day.
Endure women the sun is ending.
Women endure until the end.

Women of Soul
God has a place in your heart.
Your heavenly father is not very far.
Keep your spirit full of praise
and may your soul live every day.
Enter into the gate, God has a
beautiful heaven to live in someday.

Billie Green

Women of Wind
Capture the beauty in the air.
Your wings are so beautiful that
God can fill them in the air.
Beauty is within and never ends,
God's love is with you
every minute of the day.

Chosen Women
It is a blessing to be chosen by the Lord.
God has found favor upon many hearts,
it is truly a blessing to be chosen by the Lord.
You have so many gifts inside your heart.
It's a blessing to be chosen.

Billie Green

Tarried women that never cease to pray.
She is always a delight in a special way.
Her children praise her,
her husband adores her,
her day had no ending
and she tarried all night.
God has a special place for her.
Tarried women that never cease to pray,
always keep a special day.

Women of Violence
God came that you might have peace,
the peace to set you free.
God is a peacemaker that keeps
you all the way.
Hold on to your peace
and let God come in.
Women of violence please
don't let satan come in.
Open your heart and let
your heavenly father come in.

Billie Green

Women you are so great,
may peace and safely
guile all the way.
God's blessing is flowing
your way.
Don't be discouraged,
be patient and love
the Lord today.

Women, There is Hope
There is hope for the
things we don't understand.
Our hope is in God
that came to give us life.
There's hope for tomorrows,
please stay on your
knees and pray.

Remember, Hardships Make Us Strong
Hardships bring us
closer to the Lord.
They make us cry
and make us glad.
Hardships help us
to overcome so many rules.
God can bring us through
many trials in our life.
Remember, hardships
come to make us strong.

God Loves Us Every Moment
It's nice to know God
loves us in so many ways.
Women of the moment,
God is with you.
Let your light shine.
God's love is with us
every moment of the day.

Esther Obtained Favor of God
Esther was a strong woman
because she loved God first.
Esther obtained favor with God.
Esther was an example to all women
that God must be first.
God loved Esther because
she put God first.

Esther would not bow to king.
Now that's a great faith,
that Esther would not bow to king.
Women of faith
bow to King Jesus.
He is your saving grace,
that your life will stand.

Billie Green

There's forever hope
that we do not understand.
The hope we have in God
will always last.
There is forever hope
that we'll live forever.
In our heart God
is our blessed hope
that He's forever more.

God Brings Light to Every Man
God is the light
that never goes dim.
The strong arise in our life,
to see the light.
God is our guiding light
that brings hope and freedom.

Billie Green

God is my refuge and power.
Can't no darkness withstand God.
Shield me when I walk through
darkness at night.
I am not afraid
because God is my refuge
that guides me all day.

God is my Father
who is always by my side.
God walks with me and talks with me.
I am never alone.
I love my heavenly Father,
he always makes my day.
God my Father that makes
me smile every day knowing
I am not alone anymore.
I love my Father always.

God is Our Lord
My Lord is someone I rely upon
and someone I can pray to.
Knowing that God is my Lord
and these two are one.
I love the Lord today
because he first love me.

Women of battle,
the battle just began.
God had never lost the battle,
He had always won.
Don't get weary,
keep running the race.
There's never a battle
that God cannot win.

Billie Green

Desire Women
Desire God's blessing that
holds the power.
Desire our Saviour,
He will hold your hand.
There is a blessing
that never fades away.
Blessings come every
moment of the day
full of love and saving grace.
Open your heart,
God's love will flow in
every moment of the day.

Behold woman that
is pleasing in God's sight.
Together she stands in
God's boldness and hand,
she never loses a battle.
Victory at last,
behold the woman
so mighty at heart.
She always has a word
she kept in her heart.

Billie Green

Praying woman always
stays on her knees.
She never grows weary
because she knows God is near.
She likes the cities
that set on the hill.
She's as soft as a dove,
nothing can harm her,
so mighty and strong.
God loves a praying woman,
standing very strong.

Women of Prosperity
Your heavenly Father gives
wisdom to obtain wealth.
Hold to God's promise and
let the blessings flow.
Prosperity is never too late.
Open your heart and
let God plan your day.

Be Not Weary
Women don't get weary,
your heavenly Father wants
to bless you all the way.
Seek the Lord that He
will guide you the way.
Your husband is near,
if only you pray and
keep the faith.

Women of Virgin
so secret and dear.
God plans is to fill every
woman's need.
Hold on to your love
that's so dear.
You're beautiful as
a bumble bee.
A bee is like honey and
spice woman of virgin.
Hold on to your blessing,
for your heavenly Father is near.

Billie Green

Women, God will heal your pain.
Healing comes within your heart.
Open your heart
because God is not far.
God will heal your pain,
do not be dismayed.
Keep a smile every day
and have a blessed day.

Women, your work is not done.
God's work is never done.
Children are playing and laughing
and doing the chores.
But God's work is never done.
Oh, what delight
speak God work never end way.
Women of Smile
Don't let your smile fade away.
Your smile brightens God's day.
Let your thoughts be many
kind words to say.
Let every word be pure and divine.
Women of smile,
blessings are flowing your way.

Journeyed Women
Seek and you shall find,
God is waiting for you.
Look to God, he is right there.
There is never a mile
that is so long.
Women of journeys,
God is there,
seek and you shall find.

Deceived women never go far.
The eye of the Lord moves to and from.
Open your heart and let God rule.
Your deceived heart can be cured,
but let God's way rule.
Deceived women open your heart,
and let God's love flow.

Billie Green

Awake Women
Always be ready to pray,
always ready for God's way.
Keeping house all her children
are ready to play.
Awake women, God has a plan
to set you free.
Awake early, that pleases thee.
The birds are singing,
the bees are buzzing.
Bright and early
the prayers go forth.
Awake women,
give everything to the Lord.

Increase Women
Knowledge will never stop flowing.
Only believe that wisdom
comes from heaven above.
Never stop praying
for what you believe.
Increase women,
God's wisdom never stops
flowing from heaven above.

Billie Green

Holy women are full of God's love.
There are many gifts that God will reveal.
Holy women, her standards are nice.
She holds on her victory,
makes peace with all men.
Her heavenly Father adores
her with His hand.
There's never a sad day,
because God has her
victory in His hands.

Busy Moms
The day is full
of laughter and joy.
Leading the children
off to school.
There's never enough
time to pray.
Busy moms,
so full of joy,
give your best time
to the Lord.

Billie Green

God's Love is Perfect
What a perfect love,
so full of grace and charm.
The perfect love seems
to never pass my days.
A love I can depend upon,
A love I can call my own.

Love Blooms In Relationships
Relationships come in all kinds of forms.
God's love surrounds us, even at birth.
Love grows in our hearts as we grow older.
God's love never fades away.

There's a crown for every woman
who waits on the Lord.
Your life is hidden in Christ.
You are running a race,
in Christ you win.
There's a crown for every woman,
who's life waits on the Lord.

God's Love is Like Silver and Gold
God's love is white as snow,
silver as the shining of the stars,
gold as pure as the sun.
God's love is so warm and nice,
God's love is like silver and gold.

There is a crown
that never tarnishes,
of women of youth.
There is a crown for you
that will never tarnish.
Keep the faith and
God would open His gate.
The crown that would never
tarnish is waiting for you.

God Speaks Good News For You
Good news is everywhere,
in our jobs and in our schools.
That good news is for you and me.
Open your heart and
let God's news school you.

God's love surrounds us.
There's never an ending day,
the love that's shared with us.
At the cross he paid.
God's love is free and
surrounds us indeed.
God's love surrounds us
and there's no cost to pay.

Becoming a Mother is Wonderful
A mother's day never ends,
but God's work just begins.
Her love for her children
never passes away.
God's love is wonderful,
so peaceful and rich.
Being a mother is the
greatest love of all.

Mary was a virgin,
she was blessed of the Lord.
Mary had a baby boy,
other women were
looking for that joy.
Mary stood her test
and she wept with joy.
Mary survived with a smile
and was blessed of the Lord.

God Answers Women's Prayers
Whether or not
God answers prayers,
don't stop praying
never look down.
God is there to
answer all prayers.
Women don't stop praying
give all your burdens
to the Lord.

Woman of power
stands tall in the faith.
Her glory never fades,
her glory shines every day.
Women, stand in the victory
and always pray.
The secret of each woman
only God knows.
Stand with liberty and freedom,
always keep the victory.

Women keep a clean heart
that your love will never fade away.
Dreams will come true
if you only pray.
Your heavenly Father
loves a clean heart,
because His spirit wants
you to live in every way.

Billie Green

Hurting Women Please Don't Cry
All tears are beautiful and divine,
God will come and wipe away all tears.
Hurting women please don't cry.
God is there to comfort you.

Hopeless Women
It is never too late for you.
God has a plan for
every woman's way.
Don't give up
in things you do.
Hopeless women,
don't let the cares of
this life take you through.
God has a plan for you.

Billie Green

It takes a miracle for you and me,
it takes a miracle to make
my dreams come true.
I can see the miracle that
God has for you and me.
Miracles are real,
they never seem to fade away.
I believe in miracles
that brighten my day.

Woman, your hair is so beautiful,
your skin is so loving.
Your heavenly Father designed you perfect.
God loves you just the way you are.
The cares of this life are taken by looks.
God's love is taken by
the kindness of your ways.

Eve was the first
woman of the garden.
Eve was beautiful indeed.
God made Adam and Eve,
Adam fell asleep.
I am so glad Christ came
to set me first.

Lord make me successful,
so that I can please thee.
Lord help me to hold out,
so I can walk with thee.
Lord help me be able
to obey you so I can live free.
Lord order my footsteps so
that I may be next to thee.
Lord help me love you
every hour of every day
so that you may never flee.

Rebekah met her husband at the well.
Isaac was a blessed man.
She knew this love was very nice.
She stretched out her hand.
God found favor upon Rebekah
and gave her a perfect man,
he led her the way.
And God led them
to the promised land.

Woman of Blossom
You're like a lily or a daisy
that never grows old.
The beauty of the sun
that shines so bright,
let the glory of the Lord
shine in your life.
Woman of blossom
you're like the
Lily of God Valley
that's full of life.

Billie Green

Let God patiently
have it His way.
Work in our mysterious
ways never seem to
go very far,
even though we are trying.
In our faith
love the Lord
with all your heart.
Let God patiently live
day by day.

Sarah
Sarah was Abraham's wife.
She was 98 years old,
a blessed woman
that lived her time and
was so divine.
The angel of the Lord
said unto her
Behold, thou art with child.
Sarah was blessed of the Lord.

Billie Green

Hanna prayed unto the Lord
and all her help came from Him.
Hanna's womb was barren
and she called upon the Lord.
She never lost her faith,
Hanna had a baby boy,
oh what a wonderful day.

Women Don't Weep
God will dry up all your tears.
The joy of the Lord will come
if only you smile.
Sunny days fill your heart
with God's peace,
joy and happiness.
Any may your heavenly Father
keep you all the way.

There is a God
that never goes dry.
He's always there to carry
out each day.
Keep the praise in your heart,
there are many mountains
to climb.
Never let your praise go dry
or far apart.

God's love is full charm.
It's like sugar and spices,
so full of joy, cares and understanding.
Love is so divine.
God has all the answers
to my dreams.
Keep in mind
God is full of charm and
His love is so divine.

Billie Green

Women of faith
can move mountains.
Faith can change any day,
women of faith.
Stand bold
women of courage.
Stand free, free indeed.
God has a plan for each woman.
Women of faith,
may you have perfect peace.
Women of faith,
may you always pray.

Hopeless Woman
It is never too late for you,
God has a plan to make you
a part of heaven some day.
Don't feel down
in whatever you do.
There's always good news,
keep your faith
and don't be dismayed.
God would like to meet
you face to face.

Ruth loved her mother-in-law
with all her heart.
She didn't care if she
would ever marry again,
because God had a plan
for her life.
She did marry at the end.

God's love is everlasting.
God loves forever,
His peace gives us victory.
Please don't hide,
God's love will shine
to brighten your day.
God is caring and
full of sharing.
Troubled women
don't be dismayed.
God has a plan to
carry your burdens away.

Women, I know there are
hidden treasures that are
not very far.
Ask God for help to
open your heart.
God has the answer
too all your needs.
Trust and obey God,
He will set you free.
Free, free indeed.
Keep in mind,
your hidden treasures
are not very far.

Women, I thank God
for waking me up.
I thank God
for touching me.
I thank God
for who I am.
I thank God
for being my friend.
I say to all women
it is a honor for being
a woman who God
made especially
for His glory.

I came to love God so.
I never knew this kind of love,
so rich, so compassionate,
so caring.
I always wanted to know
this kind of love
that never fades away.
I hope to share this kind of love,
so others can know one day.
I never knew this kind of love,
so deep, warm and caring.

Women Don't Weep
God gives peace
and He will wipe
all your tears away.
Stay on your knees
and have good sleep.
God loves you in
all your doings.
Your labor is not in vain,
God will love you always
until the end of days.

Billie Green

What it means to be a wife
keep up our chores,
bathe our children,
love our husbands.
The most important
meaning is putting God first.

Pray for others
in special ways.
Christ prayed for me,
at the cross he laid.
He showed me His love
in a very special way.
I love the Lord today
because He loved me first.

Billie Green

The road to take is very straight.
God is there to guide in every way.
There is a light that shines so bright.
May your heavenly Father
lead you all the way.

Women Love Your Family
Loving our families
is not very hard.
A woman has a special heart.
Love grows inside us,
like a seed that's being planted.
God loves us with all His heart.

Women of Heart
Women let you love flow
because God's love always
wants to flow in your heart.
Love is no cost.
God's love come down
and there is not cost.
Women let your love come down,
please don't run away.
You don't have to pay,
God's love flows every day.

When you're not feeling your best,
wait on the Lord and He will heal you.
When you're feeling down,
God is there to comfort you.
When you feel all alone,
God fills your heart with love.

Women Don't Go Astray
I hope you have a perfect day.
Don't let life take control.
Blessings are upon us.
Men can't hold your back.
Women, may you have
encouragement today.

Be Content in God
It's a beautiful way to live,
knowing you have peace
and you're content in
every way you live.
Lean not on your own
understanding, be content
in God. It's the best way to live.

God Cares About Everything We Do
It's a blessing to know
that God cares about
everything we do.
That encourages me
in the things I do.
God cares when I am too busy.
I want to thank you Lord
in everything I do.

Do Not Be Afraid
God is around each
moment of the day.
When life seems to
take the best of us,
be not afraid.
God's warmth is
with you all the way.

A kind woman draws
people in her path.
She has favor with God.
She has a way with her
kind words to express.
Everybody loves her
because she really loves the Lord.

A sewing woman makes
clothes all day.
She's like the woman in
Proverbs 31, helping the needy
and her children adore her.
To be a sewing woman
you have what it takes.

A Happy Woman
She is never sad
she makes the most of her day.
She expresses her thoughts
on her happy face.
All of God's grace and love
are flowing her way.

A Singing Woman
She sings praises unto the Lord,
she never sings out of tune.
God loves her praise
because she's singing every day.
She never sings the blues,
she sings the harp of praise.

Billie Green

Thank God for His blood that
He shed for me and for you.
Thank God for the blood,
He died for me to see.
The blood that heals me,
the blood that frees me.

Woman of the Day
May your day be full of praise,
may a song be in your heart to stay.
Pray for peace and that your
heavenly Father keeps you
on your knees.
May God keep you and guide you
all the way.
Women of the day,
always keep happy praise.

Billie Green

Master Woman
Rest at your master's feet,
King Jesus can fill all your needs.
There's never a battle
too hard for God,
Just trust in the Lord.
Master woman full of grace,
there's always wisdom to learn.

Fruitful Woman
The bearing of your womb
is special in the sight of God.
Blessed is the woman
who is fruitful.
There are always blessings
flowing your way.

Billie Green

Righteous women
shall see God.
Oh what a blessed day.
God has a plan
for His way.
Never plan your day
but keep the faith,
it's never too late,
spend time to pray.
Oh what a happy day,
righteous women
always seek to pray.

Women of life stand bold
in the things you do.
There is no valley to low
that you can't go through.
Keep the faith
and may God keep you.

Billie Green

Beautiful woman
so lovable and adoring.
There's always a sweet word
to express from the kindness
of her heart.
God's beauty is so rich
and divine, all His blessings
are laying at the golden gates.
I hear the soft music
angels are playing.
Beautiful woman you are
so pleasant and adoring.

Woman of fountain
that never goes dry,
the fountain of youth
that never goes dry.
God is the river
that never goes dry.
There is a fountain
that is running freely,
there is no cost,
it's free indeed.
Woman of fountain,
God is the fountain
that never goes dry indeed.

Women of Heaven
There is a heaven so
shiny and bright.
The streets are full of gold.
The heavens are opening
for every woman today.
Keep the faith, trust and obey.
The grass is green,
the fountain is crystal clear.
Women of heaven
hold on to your faith,
and you shall freely
go one day.

Troubles Don't Last Long
Reach out to the Lord
that heals all our diseases.
Trouble is amidst.
Obey the Lord,
your troubles won't last long.

Women It's Only a Test
A test comes in all kinds of ways.
A test comes you make you strong.
Your heavenly Father will help
you every step of the way.
Be strong in the Lord and stand.
At least go through your test,
they never last.
Women, it's only a test
that soon passes away.

Women Don't Cry
God's love will dry your eyes.
Open your heart and feel God's love,
there's never an ending part.
Reading God's word
will comfort your heart.
There's no ending parts
in God's love.

Women of Heart
So tender and mild,
God's wisdom is running
freely indeed.
God holds your dreams
and many visions to see.
Women of heart,
God has the key
to open your heart.

Women of Ideas
Ideas come in many ways.
God has a plan for you.
Don't be impatient
but trust in the Lord.
Ideas are wonderful only
when we seek the Lord.

Billie Green

Women of Colors
Colors come in all shades.
God's love never changes
and is full of charm.
God's love for women
never passes away.
Our nations stand tall
with love and compassion.
God is gracious to
women of colors,
He'll never change His way.

About the Author

I am Billie Green, author of the new book *Troubled Women God Cares When You Are Hurting.* I am a mother of five children and a wife. I was writing *Troubled Women God Cares When You Are Hurting* in 1998. I went to Broadripple High School. I attended Lockyear College in 1986. I am now a writer. I had completed my first book I want to thank God for giving me a great inspirational to write my first book and share my thought with other men and women that dreams can come true only if you believe with God all things are possible to them that believe.